The Management Guide to Managing

Kate Keenan

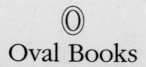

Oval Books

Published by Oval Books
335 Kennington Road
London SE11 4QE

Telephone: (0207) 582 7123
Fax: (0207) 582 1022
E-mail: info@ovalbooks.com

First published by Ravette Publishing.
This edition published by Oval Books.

First edition 1995
New edition 1999

Series Editor – Anne Tauté
Editor – Catriona Scott

Cover designer – Jim Wire, Quantum
Printer – Cox & Wyman Ltd

Cover – The prize awaits those who
take on the challenge of managing.

ISBN: 1-902825-75-6

Contents

This book is dedicated to
those who would like to manage better
but are too busy to begin.

Managing

Everyone needs to manage. Successful managing means coping with things and getting them done well enough to ensure a successful outcome. It means attainment by design rather than by chance. It makes the difference between achieving something to a satisfactory standard and not achieving anything, or only partly doing so.

Managing involves a host of disparate activities such as making plans, allocating resources, solving problems, taking decisions, directing operations and maintaining control, each one of which can seem to be an impossible mountain to climb. But when simplified, these become a series of foothills which are fairly easy to tackle once you know how.

This book describes the distance that you require to cover and the knowledge, skills and attitudes you need to develop to meet the challenge and win first prize.

★ ★ ★ ★ ★

1.   The Need for Managing

Managing well needs a little time and a bit of effort. It can be all too simple to say that things are too difficult and accept the situation stoically. Letting things drift can seem to be the easier way out, especially if you are not sure exactly what is involved in managing effectively.

Understanding the need for purposeful action is essential. But so is getting to grips with some of the stumbling blocks which can prevent you from managing to your full capacity.

Not Knowing Your Purpose

Whether you are running a church fête or an international business, managing is a great deal easier if you are sure about what it is you are expected to achieve. Unfortunately, objectives are not always clearly defined. This means you may not always know what your goals are and whether you are dissipating your efforts.

If your objectives are not obvious, you will tend to muddle along. You do what you think is required and hope that things will work out for the best. This is not the ideal recipe for achieving consistent and successful results.

People often seem reluctant to ask questions to find out what they are supposed to be achieving, possibly because to do so is seen as a sign of weakness, or worse still, stupidity.

But, if you do not fully understand your purpose, how can other people be expected to? So do not be afraid to seek clarification about what is required and take the time to work out how you can achieve what you need to achieve. If you know this, at least you can be sure the action you are taking has a purpose.

Not Being Organised

If you are not organised, it is more than likely that you are making extra work for yourself. Disorganisation means that you are not coping properly and that all your work suffers as a result. This in turn causes those people who are working with you to become frustrated and not give of their best.

Some of the symptoms which could indicate that you are disorganised might be:

- Having no plan or system, so you cannot begin to predict unexpected events and you spend your time coping brilliantly with crises which should never have happened in the first place.

- Neglecting or delaying the provision of information or materials to people who needed them urgently – probably yesterday.

- Working on a day-to-day basis, rather than looking at the whole picture, so you tackle what turns up at the time and allow less important, but often more interesting, things to get in the way of that which you should be doing.

Not being organised does not necessarily mean you are inefficient; on the contrary, you may be very good at getting things done. It is just that the things you are doing are not necessarily the right things.

Being organised is about understanding your priorities so that you do what needs to be done.

Not Seeing the Problems

Recognising that problems exist can be a problem in itself, especially if you are too close to the situation. It can be hard to see beyond your nose. There could be several reasons for this:

- If you inherit a knotty situation, you will have your work cut out just coping with things on a regular basis.

- If you are faced with too much to do, you may miss seeing the large problems because you are so busy sorting the trivial ones – a bit like rearranging the deck chairs on the Titanic.

- If you carry on doing things the way they have always been done, you may not realise that the situation has changed or that new solutions could be the answer. If you do not adapt to these changes, you may find it impossible to achieve your goals.

A large part of managing is about solving problems and making decisions. In order to do this effectively, you need to recognise that there are problems so that you know you need to seek solutions.

Not Working with People Properly

Many people think managing is about being in charge and giving orders. Telling people what to do does work, but it does not usually result in people being totally committed to doing what they have been told.

People will follow instructions, but they may not do their tasks properly. So time has to be spent enforcing instructions and keeping a firm control over all sorts of trivial things. Attitudes can develop which are difficult to deal with, such as:

- Doing the bare minimum and being unwilling to go that extra mile.

- Not paying attention to the detail required, so the job has to be done again.

- Being confused about what is expected and doing the wrong things.

If you take the trouble to indicate to people the standards required, to communicate clearly and concisely, and to show that you care about them and their work, you will find that they are more willing and much more productive.

Discussing why things need to be done means they will understand what they are expected to do and require far less supervision, with little or no enforcement.

Not Shouldering Responsibility

When things do not go as smoothly as they should, or, indeed, do not happen at all, it is much easier to blame someone or something else for this failure.

It can be very tempting to hide behind the excuse that other people did not do what they should have done or that you did not know what was going on. Unfortunately, ignorance is no excuse.

When you are in charge of getting something done,

the responsibility for the successful accomplishment of the task is always yours. If you are not prepared to be answerable for everything that comes under your control, you cannot be said to be managing.

You always have to carry the can should things go wrong, but, equally, the reward and glory is yours when things go right.

Summary: Managing Effectively

Managing is a bit like wading through a swamp. Sometimes you make quite good progress, but at other times, you find yourself surrounded by alligators or bogged down by mangroves.

When this happens, it is easy to panic and react spontaneously. It is also exceedingly easy to forget that the reason you were in the swamp in the first place was to drain it.

Being fully aware that the purpose of managing is to make things happen and achieve results is an important basic requirement if you are to do it successfully.

Questions to Ask Yourself

Think about the activities you manage and answer the following questions:

♦ Do I tend to muddle along without a purpose?

♦ Do I often hope that things will just turn out for the best?

♦ Do I forget to tell people things they need to know?

♦ Do I get side-tracked from what I should be doing by more interesting things that crop up?

♦ Do I sometimes fail to see that a problem has arisen while I'm busily occupied elsewhere?

♦ Do I often find people unco-operative when I tell them what to do?

♦ Do I tend to blame something or someone else when things are not going well?

If you have answered 'Yes' to some or all of these questions, you may need to look carefully at how you are managing.

You Will Be Doing Better If...

★ You know that you need to be clear about your purpose.

★ You can identify areas where you need to be better organised.

★ You are prepared to plan.

★ You are willing to take responsibility for what is under your control.

★ You understand the need to manage effectively.

2. Managing Functions

Managing any undertaking, such as operating a business, providing a service or running a home, involves a group of key functions which need to be performed if the desired objectives are to be realised. Managing requires that a good proportion of your time is spent carrying out some or all of the following functions:

- **Planning**: which means defining goals, forecasting, and working out schedules so that the right things are done in the right order.
- **Organising**: which means deciding what is required and who will do it, and co-ordinating.
- **Directing**: which means instructing, motivating and leading.
- **Controlling**: which means keeping an eye on things to check that everything is going according to plan.

This is a circular process; everything is held in balance and each function depends on the others being successfully executed. They form part of a cycle which is continuously repeated.

If you are to be proficient at managing, you need to to apply these functions in order to achieve your objectives – say, for example, to drain the swamp.

Planning

In order to manage well, you need to plan. This requires you to know your ultimate aim, for without a strategic overview you will find it difficult to plot precisely what has to be done. To devise a way to accomplish it, you need to know four things:

- Where you are now.
- Where you want to be.
- How you will get there.
- How you know you have got there.

Knowing what your goals are enables you to plan the work and helps you to keep heading in the right direction. Getting your priorities right sorts out what needs to be done and in what order.

Planning requires you to be skilled at:

- Analysing the current situation.
- Forecasting what has to be achieved.
- Calculating how this will be done.
- Evaluating progress and making adjustments.

This way, you will be looking at the swamp, visualising a theme park, taking stock of the problem and concluding that the swamp requires clearing; planning the best course of action, and working out a method for keeping track of progress.

Organising

In order to put your plan into action in an efficient and effective way you need to organise what you want to happen. This means dividing up the work and specifying the resources (both material and human) required to carry out the necessary tasks and allocating them correctly.

Organising means that you have to think things through carefully and determine:

- What specific tasks need to be carried out.
- Which materials you will use for each task.
- Who will carry out these tasks.

Organising requires you to be skilled at:

- Thinking logically.
- Marshalling your resources.
- Making sensible decisions.

Organising the clearance of the swamp requires you to drain the water away, round up the reptiles and remove the mangroves.

To do this you will need to make a list of what you need, then order pumps, ropes, nets, axes and shovels. You will also to need to hire a gang of able-bodied and stout-hearted people, work out their shifts, and lay on limitless sustenance.

Directing

In order to direct operations you need to provide guidance by instruction. People need direction if their actions are to be effective so it is important you ensure that everyone involved knows:

- What the overall objectives are.
- What specific things they have to do.
- What standards are expected.

Knowing the reasons why they are doing something enables people to work more efficiently and to the required standards. They can see the purpose of their actions and they are able to use their initiative more constructively.

Directing requires that your skills with people are as fully developed as the analytical skills needed when putting a plan together or organising the action. You can plan and organise until you are blue in the face, but if you do not direct operations competently, little will happen and you will end up doing it all yourself.

Directing requires you to be skilled at:

- Leading people in the right direction.
- Communicating what needs to be done.
- Motivating them to do well.

To direct the swamp operation, you need to stand

on the bank, don the cap labelled 'Boss', pick up the megaphone and issue clear and concise instructions as to what should be done.

And from time to time you need to shout morale-boosting phrases to encourage and inspire everyone to keep going, especially if it looks as if the alligators may end up outnumbering the workforce.

Controlling

In order to control all the action, you need to be adept at keeping an eye on where everything is and what is going on.

Controlling is the function by which you regulate the plan. This means steering the right course, taking corrective action, and increasing the pressure or applying the brakes when necessary.

To do this you need to:

- Understand the state of play.
- Keep an eye on the detail.
- Judge how people are performing.

Controlling requires you to be skilled at:

- Observing the action.
- Measuring performance against standards.
- Deciding on and implementing necessary action.

To control what is going on in the swamp, you have to maintain constant vigilance by being on site, with your clip-board, checking progress and performance, timescale and costs, against the original plan. You also need to apply pressure where this is needed and prevent people from doing daft or dangerous things.

Summary: Basic Managing

Managing can be broadly defined as deciding what should be done and then getting it done. Although the two activities can be thought of as separate, in practice they often overlap.

To ensure that things work, the basic functions of managing are:

- Planning what you want to do (identifying the aims and specifying everything to be carried out).
- Organising who should do what (dividing up the work and assigning the various tasks).
- Directing the action (leading, telling people what to do and getting the best out of them).
- Controlling the outcome (keeping everything regulated, on time, within estimated cost and in line with the overall plan).

In the best of all possible worlds, this is all that managing is about.

Questions to Ask Yourself

Think about the various managing functions and ask yourself the following questions:

♦ Have I made a plan to accomplish my goals?

♦ Have I identified and organised the resources I need to achieve my plan?

♦ Have I specified the tasks to be done?

♦ Have I assigned who should do what?

♦ Have I communicated what needs to be done to everybody involved?

♦ Have I stipulated the standards required for success?

♦ Am I in control of what I am doing?

You Will Be Doing Better If...

★ You are aware of what you want to achieve.

★ You make a plan to accomplish your goals.

★ You organise activities and resources so that you know who will be doing what and when.

★ You communicate what is to be done to the various people involved, and to what standards.

★ You feel you are more in control.

3. Managing Skills

To manage effectively, you need to develop a whole range of skills which at first sight appear daunting and difficult. In fact, they can all be incorporated in the following three categories:

- **Analysing skills**: solving problems and making decisions.
- **Communicating skills**: disseminating information, being assertive and running meetings.
- **Influencing skills**: leading, motivating, delegating and negotiating.

Without making the effort to polish these skills, managing will be an uphill struggle. If you do make the effort, you will be fully equipped to scale the mountain and reach the summit.

Analysing Skills

These skills help you to break down complex tasks and ideas into their component parts and examine them in detail. This means you are less intimidated by problems and more confident about deciding what needs to be done.

Solving Problems

Problems constantly arise which need to be solved. The first step in solving a problem is to recognise that one exists. It can sometimes be difficult to know where to start, so having a logical process can be helpful. These are the things you have to address:

- Diagnosing the causes of the problem. (Working out what is wrong.)
- Thinking up possible solutions. (Generating a range of options which might solve the problem.)
- Weighing up the pros and cons. (Evaluating the options.)
- Choosing the most sensible solution. (Determining the best course of action.)

By considering the pluses and minuses and allowing yourself the space and time to mull things over, the solution usually presents itself.

Making Decisions

Making decisions is an active process; it involves making choices between alternatives.

Immediate decisions usually require you to separate the urgent from the important. If you do not do this, you will find yourself spending time on minor matters, while not giving enough attention to resolving the important ones. Longer-term decisions require a basic resolution about the ultimate goal – what it is that you want to achieve. Once your purpose is clear, you can decide what to do.

It is vital to fix on a course of action and do something, rather than let things happen through hesitancy or inaction. So the key skill in making decisions is to make them.

Communicating Skills

Conveying ideas and instructions to others requires the skillful manipulation of language. To keep information flowing between yourself and others it is necessary to develop your abilities in communicating, asserting yourself and running meetings.

Communicating

Effective communication relies on the message being correctly received. Not only must your message be transmitted intelligently but the recipient must be willing to listen. This means:

- Making sure you are clear about what you want to communicate. (The idea.)

- Deciding on the method by which you will communicate your message; e.g. telephonic, electronic, on paper or in person. (The medium.)
- Composing your message in such a form that it is correctly received and understood by those for whom it is intended. (The slant.)

Communicating properly may mean repeating your message several times and in several forms. This might seem unnecessary, but it is often the only way to make sure it has been received and understood.

Asserting Yourself

Assertiveness is a technique which enables people to manage better by communicating openly and directly. It allows a message to be transmitted in a way which not only indicates what is wanted, but also inspires others to want to carry it out.

It works on two premises: that everyone has assertive rights and that everyone has a right to use these rights. This means that passive people, who are less likely to accept that they have rights, learn to speak up, and more aggressive people, who may need to appreciate that others have the same rights as they do, learn to take time to listen to others and be less judgmental.

Running Meetings

Meeting regularly is a productive way of communicating with people with whom you work closely. No matter how much you see others on a daily basis, the communication you have with them is usually informal and often about mundane issues.

A planned meeting enables you to talk about important topics in a special context. It allows you to set an agenda to discuss ideas in depth, and it gives people the opportunity to make suggestions.

When managing a meeting you need to decide before calling it what sort of meeting it is going to be; for example, whether it will be held for regular updating or called to solve a particular problem.

However, no amount of meetings can resolve anything unless they are productive. This means you have to ensure that :

- They are properly run (i.e. they start on time and people do not ramble, dominate the proceedings, or bully others).
- Everyone attending knows why they are there.
- A summary is made of what is to be done and who is to be responsible for doing it.

If you do not attend to these points, there is a good chance that meetings will not achieve anything of significance, other than arranging yet another meeting.

Influencing Skills

It is not possible to do everything yourself, nor indeed is it desirable, so a large part of managing involves getting those who work with you, or for you, to play their part in what needs to be done. Influencing skills involve being effective at leading, motivating people delegating the right tasks and negotiating.

Leading

To influence people to achieve goals, you need to work out a way of leading them that is a balance between Napoleon and Pollyanna, i.e. that the methods you use are neither too task-orientated nor too people-focused. The skills involved concern:

- Being fair and firm.
- Gaining trust in working relationships.
- Stimulating people to work well.

How you find a way of being firm and fair is up to you. It depends on your own personality and the personalities of those you lead.

Fostering good relationships and encouraging people while achieving the goals is much easier, and requires that you enthuse and support them.

If you do these things well, leading will not be a problem, nor will you lack enthusiastic followers.

Motivating

To get people going, you first need to understand what motivates them; you then need to motivate them; and finally, you need to keep them motivated.

Understanding motivation means appreciating that people have three basic needs which require to be satisfied: to earn enough to live, to feel part of a social group and to accomplish personal ambitions. But satisfying these needs does not necessarily mean that people are fully motivated.

How you treat people has a direct effect on the amount of effort they will be prepared to exert in getting things done. To get them to try extra hard, you need to:

- Give them responsibility for getting things done.
- Allow them to work in a way which suits them best.
- Praise them when they perform well.

Once people are motivated, you have to work at maintaining their momentum. You do this by:

- Watching for signs of poor morale, e.g. disaffection, disillusionment, laziness, apathy, etc.
- Being interested in them and encouraging the belief that what they are doing is worthwhile.
- Emitting a positive attitude and being consistent in your behaviour.

If you treat people decently, ensure that they are doing what they are good at, and show as much interest in them as you do in their work, you will have little difficulty in motivating them.

Delegating

To be able to delegate you have to have the confidence to entrust tasks and responsibilities to others. You need to decide what you will pass on, and to whom.

When deciding what to delegate, you can split your tasks into three categories:

- Tasks which you must delegate.
- Tasks which you should delegate.
- Tasks which you can delegate.

When deciding to whom to assign a task, you need to know the individual's capabilities and how willing that person is. Make sure that you do not give people a task they are not good at, or not equipped to do, simply because you want to get rid of it. And always make it clear that you care about the results.

It is even better if you can make sure that what you delegate allows people to enhance their skills.

Delegating effectively allows you to spend more time on managing tasks, such as planning and organising, which means things will run more smoothly.

Negotiating

Negotiating is often misunderstood. People tend to think of it as winning an argument; in fact it is about pooling common interests and achieving mutually agreed solutions. To be successful at negotiating you need first to determine your requirements and place them in order of priority under these headings:

- **The Maximum** – what you would ideally like.
- **The Minimum** – what you must achieve if there is to be any agreement at all.
- **The Trade off** – where you would be prepared to make concessions, if pressed.
- **The Fall-back position** – your alternative action if an agreement is not possible.

You start the negotiating process by describing what you are seeking to achieve. Follow this by:

- Listening to what others have to say and asking for clarification if you are not sure what is proposed.
- Identifying where there is common ground.
- Looking for solutions which both of you might be prepared to accept.

To resolve different points of view, compromise is often the answer. Successful negotiation is not about winning and losing. The end object is for both people to feel satisfied with the result.

Summary: Managing in Practice

In practice, managing means tackling complex situations, and developing specific skills to meet these demands.

Analysing involves solving problems and making decisions. For this you need to identify that a problem exists, uncover the cause and work out a way to overcome it. You then need to make a decision as to which action to take – and take it.

Communicating is the life-blood of managing. Unless you possess the gift of thought transference, you need to communicate simply and clearly what it is you want. Being able to assert yourself ensures that social encounters are productive.

Influencing involves leading by example, motivating individuals to perform better, delegating things which can be done by someone other than yourself and negotiating agreements.

All are key skills in enabling you to get things done.

Questions to Ask Yourself

Think about your skills in managing and answer the following questions:

♦ Do I know how to diagnose problems?

♦ Do I make decisions?

♦ Do I take action to implement my decisions?

♦ Do I communicate intelligently?

♦ Do I understand that I have assertive rights?

♦ Do I know what my meetings are for?

♦ Do I lead people in a firm and fair way?

♦ Do I motivate people to want to work better?

♦ Do I delegate the right things to the right people?

♦ Do I appreciate that negotiating is not about winning?

♦ Do I feel I am developing the necessary skills to manage more effectively?

You Will Be Doing Better If...

★ You diagnose the problems and work out the options.

★ You make decisions, rather than letting things slide.

★ You take action as a result of your decisions.

★ You communicate properly.

★ You use your assertive rights to manage better.

★ You always know the purpose of the meetings you arrange and attend.

★ You inspire people to want to follow you.

★ You motivate people to want to work better.

★ You delegate effectively.

★ You are prepared to compromise when negotiating.

★ You feel confident that you can tackle all the skills which managing demands.

4. Managing Contingencies

In real life, things do not happen in an ideal way, so much of your time will be spent in having to take corrective action – righting wrongs, going backwards over things, readjusting or making day-to-day changes.

It may seem as if you are constantly damming the dyke, that no sooner have you overcome one problem than another one is lurking just around the corner.

The sort of contingencies that are likely to require managing are:

- **Resolving conflict**: which requires differences to be settled.
- **Coping with change**: which requires continuous adaptation.
- **Handling stress**: which requires excessive pressures to be recognised and reduced.

How you cope with these vicissitudes determines your expertise in managing.

Resolving Conflict

Differences of opinion inevitably arise between people. Sometimes these can be easily resolved by rational discussion; on other occasions, conflict can occur.

Conflict usually diminishes performance. If it is not resolved, bad feelings usually get worse and the situation can rapidly get out of hand.

There are several things you can do to promote the resolution of conflict:

- Remind people of the overall objectives. This allows people to see beyond their immediate concerns.
- Play down the differences and emphasise common interests between conflicting parties.
- Persuade those involved to give up something in order to come to an agreement.

It is important that serious disputes are settled if goals are to be met. Managing conflict enables people to re-focus on the overall aims, prevents things from getting worse and gets people back on course.

Managing Change

However well you might be managing, there are always changes to contend with.

It is important to bear in mind that, although you would to prefer to carry on as usual, there are many forces and influences which are outside your direct control.

Some of the longer-term changes involve:

- Political changes.
- Greater competition, both at home and abroad.
- The speed of the development of new products and new methods of production.
- The growth of information technology in all fields.

Keeping up with changes requires a positive attitude in order to see the opportunities which new situations can offer. You also need to be more receptive and not hide-bound by tradition.

Coping with change means:

- Keeping an open mind.
- Not being afraid of change.
- Letting people know where things are changing, the reasons for this, and what it means to them.
- Getting people involved in change.
- Making sure people are equipped to cope with change through briefing and training.

You need to appreciate that change of any kind can have a profound effect on individuals.

It is essential that you encourage an atmosphere of co-operation, because the greater the changes you have to cope with, the more important human relations become.

Changes will happen whether you like it or not. So you need to develop a flexible approach and adapt to changes rather than resist them.

Handling Stress

If the pressure of dealing with contingencies becomes excessive, people may eventually end up suffering from stress, though they are often the last ones to know this. Stress is the basic survival instinct which is invoked when a threat is perceived. It takes the form of a sequence of responses which prepare the body either to defend itself or to flee from the scene.

Initially stress is generated by external forces, such as work pressures and life events. Internal driving forces become exaggerated, and rather than enhancing performance can frustrate it. For instance, a drive for perfection can go overboard, leading to mistrust of other peoples' abilities and insistence on doing everything, thereby compounding stress levels.

Reducing stress is a two-stage process. First you have to reduce the immediate symptoms of stress by getting the brain back into neutral gear so that you can think more clearly and logically. You can do this by:

- Breathing deeply to get oxygen into the brain and thus overriding the stress response.
- Relaxing and letting your body come back to its normal state.

Second, you need to identify and implement strategies which assist in the reduction of stress on a longer-term basis. You do this by:

- Re-examining the way you are living your life and working out how to live more healthily.
- Getting rid of the stress hormones by taking regular exercise.

Knowing how to handle stress in a constructive way gives you the means of coping with most of the pressures that life can throw at you.

Summary: Managing the Unexpected

Resolving conflict, being receptive to change and being able to handle personal stress all play an active part in managing.

Disputes should always be addressed promptly if you are to ensure that they do not escalate. Change is a constant factor and rising to meet it, rather than refusing to accept it, is an integral part of managing. And handling stress is a key strategy in making the unexpected less intimidating, as well as providing the wherewithal to manage better.

Coping with contingencies as they occur means that you spend less time putting things right and have more time to work constructively.

Questions to Ask Yourself

Think about managing contingencies and answer the following questions:

♦ Do I attempt to resolve conflict immediately?

♦ Am I prepared to embrace and accept change?

♦ Do I recognise that stress is so much a part of everyday life that it needs to be handled continuously?

♦ Am I able to cope with contingencies as a matter of course?

You Will Be Doing Better If...

★ You settle disputes swiftly and do not defer dealing with them.

★ You are willing to adapt to changes.

★ You are taking regular exercise to reduce the effects of stress.

★ You accept that managing means coping with contingencies.

5.   Managing People

Managing of any sort requires dealing with people to some degree. Indeed, managing has been defined as the 'ability to get things done through other people'.

When managing people, a number of specific skills are brought into play:

- **Selecting**: which means ensuring you have the right people to do the required tasks.
- **Assessing**: which means appraising their abilities and competence.
- **Training**: which means providing them with the opportunities to develop relevant skills.
- **Team building**: which means using their personal attributes to best advantage.
- **Counselling**: which means assisting them to solve the problems impairing their performance.
- **Understanding behaviour**: which means appreciating the reasons behind their different viewpoints.

Once the right people are in position and functioning properly through adequate assessment and training, they can get on with the things they are meant to be doing. And if you are able to understand the reasons why they think and behave as they do, and can help them to help themselves, you will be able to get on with the things you are meant to be doing.

Selecting People

To choose the right person for a job requires thorough advance preparation. This means:

- Describing the job on offer.
- Specifying the person best suited to it.
- Advertising and making up a shortlist of the best of those who apply for the job.
- Interviewing candidates to find out more.
- Deciding which person best fits the job.

Defining the job is crucial, but so is listing the qualities required in the person who would be ideal for the job. To match one to the other you need to interview a limited number of the most likely candidates.

The key skills when interviewing involve asking the right questions and listening carefully to the answers. Much depends on the kind of questions you ask, so they have to be sufficiently well-prepared to elicit the facts and details you need when later assessing the information gathered and making the final choice.

When you select a new person you are taking one of the most important managing decisions you ever have to face. If you select the wrong person, it can have dire consequences, so it is worth the effort to prepare in a professional way. This gives you the best possible chance of getting it right.

Assessing

It is by assessing performance that people learn how well they are doing. This can give a great sense of achievement and completion, and can act as a catalyst to better performance.

Assessing involves:

- Checking how well people are doing their jobs, their skills and underlying knowledge.
- Comparing their skills and knowledge against pre-determined standards.
- Deciding whether their performance matches the standards required.

To get the best from assessing people, you need to hold formal discussions with the agreement of the individuals concerned. It is never a question of catching them out.

It is also important that the designated standards have been clearly defined, and that you have talked about what will be required before any assessment takes place.

When talking about performance it is essential to do so in a way that encourages people to keep on doing what they do well, and to instigate improvements in those areas where that which they are doing may not be up to scratch.

Training

Providing training enables people to develop their skills so that they can work more easily to the required standards as well as become better qualified.

This means:

- Identifying and agreeing the specific development.
- Finding and providing the right methods to do so.
- Monitoring and assessing the individual's learning and practical progress.

Encouraging people to want to learn is an important part of managing and motivating them. People learn best by doing, so you have to ensure that the training allows people to learn actively rather than simply absorbing information like a spectre at the feast.

It is by helping people perform their tasks better that they are able to take more pride and pleasure in their work and make a positive contribution to getting things done.

Building a Team

Managing often involves building a team of people who work together to achieve a common purpose. Effective teams are those where people not only know what they are working to achieve but also get the chance to examine their roles and personalities. The most productive team is that which consists of people who carry out complementary functions. There are four important roles which contribute to team effectiveness:

- The Leaders: people who drive the team forward to get things done to standard and on time.
- The Doers: people who put plans into action and ensure that things get done.
- The Thinkers: people who work out new ways of doing things.
- The Carers: people who look after the team, either by fixing things with those outside the team or making sure that internal relations are harmonious.

By identifying the different talents people can bring to the group you can ensure the best results.

If there are only two in the team, it is best if one is a Doer and the other a Thinker, so that ideas which are produced are actually carried out.

But whatever the size, people's responsibilities should reflect the roles to which they are best suited if the team is to be fully productive.

Counselling

Various trials and tribulations can affect people's performance, but you can assist them to work out a solution to their troubles by counselling them.

Spotting the change in behaviour which signals that all is not well can be fairly easy. It is not so easy to find out what has caused the change. You need to discuss this to see what can be done to improve the situation. By talking things over, you can help people by:

- Clarifying the situation and defining the cause.
- Prompting them to come up with useful suggestions as to how they can help themselves.
- Making temporary adjustments to working practices which may help resolve their predicament.

Getting to the root of the problem is central to sorting it. It is not incumbent upon you to solve the problem. The key to counselling is to enable people to come up with their own solutions. You may be able to help them by adjusting their work, perhaps altering the hours for a while to alleviate domestic difficulties. But whatever help is given, you need to check how the individual is coping. Above all, you need to keep the content of your discussions confidential, otherwise no-one will ever trust you with personal matters.

Developing the skills to help and support people is important. If they are not doing their jobs properly, you need to know why. It is not that you are nosy, it is simply that their failure to perform to standard is your concern. And unless you know the cause, you cannot help them.

Understanding Behaviour

Managing people is made easier if you can develop a better understanding of how others see things and why they do what they do. This means that you will become more effective in accommodating their behaviour.

How people interpret the world about them is heavily influenced by their personal characteristics and their range of experiences. Because they do things differently from you, there are several reasons why, when observing people's behaviour, you may misinterpret it.

For example:

- You only see what you want or expect to see.
- You jump to conclusions because you do not have enough information.
- You let you own views affect your perception.

To understand the behaviour of others you need to put yourself in their place. To do this you have to:

- Listen carefully to what they tell you.
- Try to see the situation as they do.
- Be interested in their values and views.

By taking the trouble to understand behaviour, you are less likely to fall into the trap of making assumptions about why people behave as they do. You will be able to accommodate more easily views and behaviour that are different from yours.

The most difficult aspect of all is that which requires you to get others to change their behaviour, but this is made a good deal easier if you can help the people concerned to understand their own.

Summary: Working with People

How well you work with people is critical: it is through their efforts that things get done.

By selecting the best people for the work; assessing levels of performance; providing the opportunities for training, and building team spirit, you enable people to understand how they fit in and what is expected of them.

Managing people also requires you to support them. This involves seeing their point of view and helping them to solve their problems as difficulties arise.

Your ability to manage people is increased ten-fold if you take a genuine interest in them. If you are prepared to develop your capacity to understand and accommodate behaviour, you will find that managing people provides mutually enriching rewards.

Questions to Ask Yourself

Think about how you manage people and answer the following questions:

♦ Do I understand the importance of selecting the right people?

♦ Do I view assessing people's performance as a way of helping them to perform better?

♦ Can I pinpoint what training may be needed?

♦ Do I ensure that any team effort uses people's talents to best effect?

♦ Am I willing to listen to other people's troubles?

♦ Do I appreciate other people's points of view?

♦ Do I make an effort to fathom behaviour?

♦ Do I consider that working with people is an essential part of managing?

You Will Be Doing Better If...

★ You prepare professionally when selecting people.

★ You regularly assess performance.

★ You provide training when and if it is needed.

★ You ensure that a team can produce its best work according to its individual aptitudes.

★ You help people define and resolve their difficulties.

★ You make an effort to understand why people behave the way they do.

★ You are willing to see things from their point of view.

★ You find that managing others is very rewarding.

6. Managing Attitudes

Managing is an attitude of mind. Hazards lurk in unexpected places, like alligators in swamps, and to keep going requires resilience and optimism, as well as a positive frame of mind. Managing successfully means taking a positive approach to:

- **Managing yourself**: ensuring that you are able to take on the rigours of managing.
- **Making time**: working to use the time available wisely, so you leave some for yourself.
- **Managing others**: working with other people to everyone's advantage.

It is your attitude to these three aspects of managing which enables you to keep going when the going gets tough.

Managing Yourself

Managing means managing yourself as well as all the other things for which you are responsible. If you do not spend some time looking after yourself, it is unlikely anyone else will and if you not give permission to take time off, you will end up on a treadmill.

There are several things you need to work out if you are to manage yourself effectively. For example:

- Deciding what you want to achieve.
- Taking charge of yourself.
- Leading a balanced life.

Planning your own direction is as important as planning the general direction you have for your work. If you do not pay attention to identifying what you want to achieve from a personal point of view, you will almost certainly not achieve it.

You need to take charge of yourself by limiting your responsibilities. It is important that you do not take on too much so that you can concentrate more on what you should be doing.

Above all, it is important that you balance your life between work and play, so that you get the best from both.

If you can do all this, you will not only gain from a personal point of view, but you will be more effective at managing.

Making Time

Managing requires that you use the time you have available to best advantage. Using time wisely means allocating your time. You need to know which things are top priority for the day, week or month. This may require you to spend a little time on the following:

- Allocating your time during the day in order to make the best use of it.
- Looking for things that waste your time and making sure that you stop doing them.
- Utilising the time spent on trains, planes, buses, etc., by doing something useful.
- Scheduling time for thinking about important things, such as future plans, next week's meeting, or for making decisions about how to use your time.

You must value your time to make the most of it. It is useful to acknowledge that you cannot work flat out all the time. You need to take time to recharge your batteries which means giving yourself permission to take time off.

Managing Others

Your attitude to people is pivotal in ensuring that they produce the results required. How you view them forms a basis for determining the way you go about managing them.

There are two distinct and contrasting views which tend to be held:

- The **negative** view: that people do not like work, and that pressure and control needs to be exerted over them if they are to do anything at all.

- The **positive** view: that people enjoy work and are willing to get on with it provided it appears meaningful and they are personally involved.

You have the choice about which attitude to take. By and large productive relationships are formed through mutual trust and respect. If your view of people is negative, such relationships are unlikely to develop. Since managing to a large extent involves getting things done through other people, it would appear that the positive approach is the most fruitful.

Summary: Enjoying Managing

If you can manage yourself half as well as you manage everything else, you will find it a great deal easier to take all that is thrown at you.

Making the best use of your time enables you to get things done and being interested in other people is essential if you are to get the best from them.

It is important that you have a positive attitude to managing if you are to meet the challenge and achieve results.

Questions to Ask Yourself

Think about how you could manage better and answer the following questions:

♦ Am I spending enough time managing myself?

♦ Do I have a clear idea of my own personal direction?

♦ Am I balancing my work with leisure interests?

♦ Have I organised myself properly?

♦ Do I know precisely what I spend my time doing?

♦ Am I allocating my time?

♦ Am I choosing to take a positive attitude towards others?

♦ Am I enjoying managing?

You Will Be Doing Better If...

★ You take the time to manage yourself.

★ You work out your personal direction.

★ You limit your responsibilities.

★ You feel you are more in control of yourself.

★ You allocate your time.

★ You improve your relationships with others.

★ You enjoy managing.

Check List for Managing

If you are finding that managing is proving more difficult than you thought, think about whether it is because you have failed to take account of one or more of the following aspects:

Understanding the Functions

If managing is proving to be harder work than you anticipated, it may be that you have not fully understood the functions of planning, organising, directing and controlling, and their importance in getting things done. It could be that you are reacting to events rather than working in a planned and structured way to make things happen. If you have a plan, organise your resources, and spend time monitoring how things are working in practice, you will feel more in control.

Getting to Grips with the Skills

If you find you are not achieving very much, it may be that you do not know how to implement your plan or organise your resources. Or it may be because you have not realised that the skills of analysing, communicating and influencing others are crucial if you are to accomplish anything. It is important you appreciate that managing is a discipline in its own right and spend time developing the skills.

Coping with Contingencies

If you expect everything to go according to plan, you may resent having to cope with contingencies. It may be that you are not addressing conflict in the hope it will resolve itself. Perhaps you are reluctant to accept change. Or possibly you are not practising stress-reducing techniques and are not in sufficient shape to deal with difficult or unpredictable circumstances.

Getting the Best from People

If you have not appreciated that you need to help people to perform better, you may not be getting the best from them and could be finding it difficult to get things done. It may be that you tend to take a negative attitude to people, rather a positive one. If you can adopt the right attitude and gain the trust of the people who work with you, you will find that getting things done is much easier.

Managing Better

If you sometimes feel that managing is an impossible task, this may be because you are not managing yourself effectively. You may be taking on too much by not delegating things to others or you may not be managing your time sensibly. Spend some time on managing yourself and everybody will benefit.

The Benefits of Managing

Managing is part of life. It is about making the best of all the resources you have at your disposal. It is almost inevitable that whatever you do, directing a business, organising a home, or running a professional practice, you will be involved in managing. And you need to do this well.

The benefits of managing successfully are that:

- You will get practical problems solved.
- You will make significant decisions.
- You will overcome obstacles.
- You will effect real changes.
- You will be able to handle pressure.
- You will enable other people to be productive and motivated.
- You will positively influence events and people.
- You will get satisfaction from what you do.

If you do not manage well, you will spend a disproportionate amount of your time and energy wrestling, sorting, coping, guiding, battling, manipulating and trouble-shooting. The trick is to manage well enough for it to become invisible, to go on in the background without impinging on the real business of life – all the things you need to be doing, other than managing.

Glossary

Here are some definitions in relation to Managing.

Assessing – Evaluating skills objectively against agreed standards.

Communicating – Transmitting instruction, thought or information so that it is properly received and understood.

Controlling – Monitoring to ensure things happen as planned and correcting any significant deviations.

Counselling – Giving help to people to help themselves.

Delegating – Allocating tasks, along with authority and responsibility.

Directing – Conducting and giving orders so that everyone knows what is happening.

Handling Stress – Keeping pressure at bay by taking regular exercise and learning to relax.

Influencing – Inducing people to want to do what is required.

Leading – Inspiring people to follow by the power of personality and recognisable expertise.

Making decisions – Committing to a chosen course of action.

Making Time – Making full use of time so as to do do more than you thought you could.

Motivating – Creating a positive working atmosphere to encourage extra effort.

Negotiating – Bargaining for a mutually advantageous outcome.

Organising – Co-ordinating or arranging in a methodical way.

Planning – Plotting ways of taking action prior to putting them into practice.

Selecting people – Choosing the right people for the job.

Solving Problems – Evaluating options and settling for the most sensible.

Succeeding – Being victorious in achievement; the ultimate triumph.

The Author

Kate Keenan is a Chartered Occupational Psychologist with degrees in affiliated subjects (B.Sc., M.Phil.) and a number of qualifications in others.

She founded Keenan Research, an industrial psychology consultancy, in 1978. The work of the consultancy is fundamentally concerned with helping people to achieve their potential and make a better job of their management.

By devising work programmes for companies she enables them to target and remedy their managerial problems – from personnel selection and individual assessment to team building and attitude surveys. She believes in giving priority to training the managers to institute their own programmes, so that their company resources are developed and expanded.

She fully understands the problems of managing. She also knows that when things go well, the satisfaction of achieving results is worth every ounce of energy and every inch of effort.

THE MANAGEMENT GUIDES

'Especially for people who have neither the time nor the inclination for ploughing through the normal tomes...'

The Daily Telegraph

Asserting Yourself

Delegating

Handling Stress

Making Time

Managing

Managing Yourself

Motivating

Negotiating

Planning

Running Meetings

Selecting People

Understanding Behaviour

These books are available from your local bookshop or from the publishers:

Oval Books, 335 Kennington Road, London SE11 4QE
Telephone: (0207) 582 7123; Fax: (0207) 582 4887;
E-mail: info@ovalbooks.com